PRAISE FOR THE POETRY OF JEFF MANN:

"This is not the sweetness and light of foamy poetry composed only of sparkles and metrics. Sweetness, yes: but the sweetness of honeysuckle or wild mint. And light, surely: but the kind of light that teases out every crease and crevice in the poet's face, a hard-edged and truthful light rather than the sort that softens and flatters. Little wonder then that his poetry has drawn comparison to the likes of John Keats, Emily Brontë, and T. S. Eliot."

—*Edge San Francisco*

"Passionate, assertive, tender, masculine, and wholly attentive to our place in and of this world, here are poems of a kindred spirit...."

—RON MOHRING, author of *Survivable World*

"I found myself feeling pride at reading such a masterful collection of gay poems, at the sense that we'd finally reached a moment where our poets could write the truth that has so long been withheld. Two centuries ago, one of our proto-gay forebears, Karl Heinrich Ulrichs, argued that gay love is natural because it exists in nature. For Mann, it is nature itself."

—DAN VERA, author of *Speaking Wiri Wiri*

A
Romantic Mann

A Romantic Mann

⁓

Jeff Mann

⁓ LETHE PRESS
MAPLE SHADE, NEW JERSEY

A ROMANTIC MANN
Copyright © 2013 Jeff Mann. ALL RIGHTS RESERVED.
No part of this work may be reproduced or utilized in
any form or by any means, electronic or mechanical,
including photocopying, microfilm, and recording,
or by any information storage and retrieval system,
without permission in writing from the publisher.

Published in 2013 by Lethe Press, Inc.
118 Heritage Avenue, Maple Shade, NJ 08052 USA
lethepressbooks.com / lethepress@aol.com
ISBN: 978-1-59021-156-4 / 1-59021-156-1

Acknowledgments for previous publication appear on
pages 121-122, which constitute an extension of this
copyright page.

Set in Warnock and LTC Metropolitan.
Cover and interior design: Alex Jeffers.
Cover image: Vintage, photographer unknown.

For John Ross, Cynthia Burack, and Laree Martin.

For Steve Berman and Ron Suresha.
Many thanks for years of friendship and support.

Many thanks to Alex Jeffers
for producing another handsome book.

Contents

One	1
Grendel	3
Snow Meal	5
The Failed Romantic Contemplates Suicide	6
Erotic Letter	8
Mysteries	9
Getting a Piece	10
Lunar Eclipse	11
Single Men	12
Galatoire's	13
The Men of Taco Bell	15
Milkweed Pods in November	17
The Failed Romantic Discovers Amy's Hot Pepper Relish	18
Sycamore	20
Romantic Weekend	22
Graveyard Maples After Sleet	24
The Failed Romantic Seduces a Blueberry Bar;	25
Relic	27
Two	31
Aeolian	33
Locrian	35
Ionian	38
Dorian	41
Phrygian	43
Lydian	46
Mixolydian	48

THREE	51
September Sunlight	53
September Morning Fog	55
Sugar Maples in October	57
Black Windows	60
4x4	62
Writers' Tour of Kayford Mountain	66
Greg's Party	68
Three Crosses	69
Alan Turing Memorial—Manchester	71
Virginia Fantasia	77
Tulip Trees, Virginia Tech	81
Sheath	83
Feasting in the Aftermath	86
Sunday Morning Biscuits	88
Anniversary	91
Star Magnolia, a Celtic Tattoo	93
FOUR	95
Achilles and Patroclus	97
Mummy Case—Fitzwilliam Museum, Cambridge	100
Gloucester Cathedral	102
Cernunnos Tattoo	104
Heaven's Hearth	106
Honeys	108
Oasis	110
Mallory Square	112
The Sexiest Man in Europe	114
Homomonument, Amsterdam	116
The Bells of Bruges	118

One

GRENDEL

I always enter the smoky hall after dewfall,
my fingers like black thongs, shaking the frost
from my beard. The bodies of men I want
are light made flesh, each conscious
of his beauty even in sleep, torsos
rising and falling in the dark,
the last crumbling oak-ember light
ashimmer in red-gold chest hair, lips
still sweet with too much mead.

Who drives me to this?
I lower myself to lance the opposite,
to stretch muscle beneath me,
to stain my lips and salt the back
of my throat. One touch, one taste
to wash the moor and the mist
from my mouth. Then the light
sees the shadow that mounts him
and rips my arm off at the roots.

I sit in this cave now
making stars out of blood clots, fingering
on the blank wall circles and petroglyphs,
while the oak roots tickle my ears.
All winter I stiffen, half-asleep,

M

my lust for that red-gold light, those
heroic chest-pelts, banked like meadhall embers.
In here I hear nothing, I trust nothing
but my own wound. And at my side,

it grows back. Cursed as a subterranean
salamander, the arm grows back,
twisted and taloned but
it grows back, aching all the way,
unfolding the same loving claws,
the same desperate dreaming for muscle
to close on as a black thong dreams
of a wrist, hell-bulb gnarling towards
the cave mouth and the northern spring.

SNOW MEAL

"The mills of the gods," the phrase
has it. Tonight they grind slowly
in nimbostratus, a flour flecking
the dead and delicate grass culms,
a sheet pulled over a face.

The long-alone in middle age
admit the truth at last: solitude
so flawless—symmetrical and unique
as a snowflake's six quartzose spears—
is a career, a mythos not likely to end.
Despite the personal ads, the afternoons
borrowed in May with married men—

the long-alone learn to live on snow
meal. In the dark the drifts
pile up like wind-kneaded loaves
of bread. Crumbs off the paten,
these sharp motes on the tongue.
Love no one wants disintegrates;
manuscripts, cave-hoarded, dryrot.
This dust we taste will wean us of the earth.

THE FAILED ROMANTIC CONTEMPLATES SUICIDE

Upon the mossy breakwater the damned
and darksome poet stands, filming himself,
having seen *The French Lieutenant's Woman*.
His long black coat wind-flaps about him.
Waves smash on either side,
sucking down the Sussex shingle
with a rattle, lapping almost to his feet.

The sea's hunger is his own.
He's parlayed yearning into a career,
an addiction to the inaccessible
drowning any urge for peace. Abrading
his oyster innards, the giggling
of tourists on the beach behind him,
the squeal and clang of the Brighton pier.
It's *Wuthering Heights* he wants,

that kind of focus, but he manages love
only once a decade, people are such bores.
He would leap now, but who would
write his elegy better than he?
He plucks at his collar and wonders
how did Heathcliff avoid lint?
The water here is polluted anyway,
the sky the color of bruises

his last lovemaking with another's spouse
left along his left thigh. Off to
his favorite pub, the Queen's Head,
to write a lyric about his suicide:

found drowned, the ring his illicit lover
gave him still on his wrinkled hand,
his belly full of prawns and Somerset cider,
a few plucked nettles and a copy
of Marcus Aurelius in his raincoat pocket.
"He has a handsome face"—so would sigh
some beautiful, unmet passerby.

EROTIC LETTER

We make love
through the mail. I lie
in bed alone, a letter
in one hand. Snow flurries
powder the window panes.
Eyes closed, I enter
your scribbled fantasies,
tying your hands behind you,
bending you over the altar.

Tonight I touch myself
as if I were you.
Odd combination:
semen on a belly,
tears in a beard.

MYSTERIES

beyond the reach of metaphysics:

an October night, the shiver of wind in yellow
    maple leaves;

resin popping on the hearth, firelight
    on your brow;

the swirled patterns of fur, soft and black,
    across your belly and chest,
        buttocks and back.

GETTING A PIECE

Tanned pectorals on Mount Diablo,
pierced nipples in Richmond,

roped wrists in West Virginia,
furry buttocks in D.C.

Cathedral sackers shatter
the stained glass.

Denied love, we chant,
bored or lonely,

these litanies of lust.
"Getting a piece."

Exactly.
Always withheld,

the whole.

LUNAR ECLIPSE

Utter silence, save for the cadaver-
restlessness of pin oak leaves
in this wind twisting into winter,
into singular shivering. Orion
coursing stilly over the chimneys
is a geometry of chinks
whose axioms escape us. This is
the cave we have learned to live in.
Now, so slowly, across the door
the stone is rolled, so slowly
the savior's eyelids shut.
Age is this gradual,
the sea's molars grinding Land's End.
Now all the earth is between
our eyes and the light, dense
with all that can never be born.

SINGLE MEN

These are the skills of frontiersmen:
cutting through laurel hells, clearing
a few hundred feet of virgin forest,
piling stones, plowing too-steep slopes,
borrowing warmth not from bodies but
burning wood. At night we heat rocks
for our beds, listen to the screech owl
shiver down our spines. Blue-green
hill-haze, mountain horizon a line
of breakers, crags rain-pitted, hemlocks
wind-flagged, year arching after year.
Every tool we must make ourselves,
every day we carve alone,
the masters of making do.

GALATOIRE'S

(for Katherine Soniat)

Begin with a Sazerac. With dinner,
Chardonnay. As appetizer, oysters
en brochette—bacon's flattery,
the crisp-fried coating, the soft gray hearts.
Then seafood-stuffed eggplant, bulging

with crabmeat and bits of shrimp.
French bread to chase each stray morsel
about the plate. Crème caramel to finish,
richer than many remembered kisses.
How many novels and movies brought

you here? You are finally fiction
for an hour or so, pushing aside
the plates now, settling back, sipping wine.
Street grime and humidity, inadequate
reality's left at the door. And the empty

chair across from you? That ripest
fruit of fiction? Lovers
who could have been here?
Long ago exposed, damned, dismissing
or dismissed. Here no one's needed.

Conversation would be distraction.

Put down the empty glass, pull out
the credit card, rise. End this lyric
of elitist elegance with a short,
muttered hedonist's prayer:

*Thanks for delights needing no one's
consent, delights those alone
can arrange themselves. Thanks for
the blessings of crabmeat and bourbon,
those joys too sweet to be shared.*

THE MEN OF TACO BELL

Some of us are ugly and we know it—
this bucktoothed scarecrow hunched over
his soft taco, this blond-bearded slab

with a dog's underbite snapping up
Spanish rice. Some of us are old—
this octogenarian quavering over

his refried beans, shuffling towards
the bathroom. Others, like myself,
for instance, are convinced we're darkly

handsome, but cursed somehow
with invisibility, too exceptional
for any save our equals. Whatever

the reason—age or looks or lack
of luck—the divorced, the abandoned,
those who've loved without success,

we eat here alone. It's a change
from microwave and television,
or the too-much-trouble of cooking

for one. In Taco Bell, there are the young

and beautiful to admire and envy giggling
in their cliques, the slow rain to watch

stippling and clawing the glass, sheening
the storm-wet streets. We eat slowly
to put off heading home. We plan

how to fill our evenings. We undress
burrito supremes and fajita wraps
from their coy paper clothing. The tortillas

resist our teeth, then yield like skin.

MILKWEED PODS IN NOVEMBER

Across those shiver-seas
of pasture, we are boats

bearing silver, silver summer
refines from mud, a school of fish

whose scales unravel now in wind.
Passion was our passenger,

but by November we have docked.
The crowded pulse of seeds

has scattered. The little bellows
puff their smoke like autumn

chimneys, then cease. In the after-
shudder, molten opals pool

in belly hair, for a moment only
the last breath mists the mirror.

What peace to be so empty.

THE FAILED ROMANTIC DISCOVERS AMY'S HOT PEPPER RELISH

I will be the first to admit
being a romantic has gotten me
nowhere, and now it's too late
to die young. I've worn black
for years, cultivated the silver
in my beard, stridden about waste
places and cliff edges. Barnabas,
Tristan, Heathcliff showed me
the way, falling in love with
all the wrong people, poems
in the true troubadour tradition.
What envy any intensity
inspires in me—the tulip's
explosions, the sugar maple's
red-orange fireball, the thunder-
storm's swagger. It's exhausting,
really, emulating such drama.

My sister chops hot peppers,
both Hungarian and cayenne,
canning a new relish to spice up
all the cold weather to come.
Soon, bright seedy crimson
smoulders atop bratwurst
or brown beans, polenta or

potato cakes. Grand passion,
I have found it at last, burning
the tongue, sweating the scalp.
Sweet and hot, like swallowed
sparks, someone else's spouse.

SYCAMORE

1
After an evening of four Bushmills, one Dewar's
neat, cautiously reattain, with morning, any
vertical. Sit on the bed's edge, cupping
your head like a cracked obsidian sphere
in which you scry every passion you ever felt
was unreciprocated, therefore trivial.

2
In the mountain coves, the last snow lingers.
All the ice you swallowed like a panacea
crystallizes along the mizmaze banks of tiny
creeks, a sidewinder meander any man caught
in body might envy. Solids weary us—
in the arms of someone long loved,
we turn to water, we turn to steam.

Along those streams—Lick Creek, Laurel Run—
the sycamores lift. They spread
their limbs like the ghosts of dowsers,
saying *Here. Press your mouth to the earth
here.* The morning after a hard Celtic
drunk, attachments peel off like sycamore bark.
You stand naked by what cold has left of
purling, your arms lifted, frost feathering

the black grass across your belly and chest.

3

Outlive all you love: the leaving will be easier.
Soon soil will melt and leave only
snow, someone you have never met will wash
your bone-shards with wine. Hold ice-edged hands
up to the light—arithmetics hard and incorruptible,
sycamore twigs the week before their budding.

ROMANTIC WEEKEND

Back to back in bed again,
each wishing the other were another.

Weekending in this romantic farmhouse,
beneath this romantic quilt. Outside

the wind chimes are whipped too manic
to make a tune, the silver maple—

fast growth, soft wood—loses a limb
in these gusts punchbagging the house.

Night after night,
I am tired of always being the first

to touch. Two lovers who left us
are laughing at the bed's foot, shimmering

like heat-ghosts over August asphalt.
Their features zigzag, distort

in the cross drafts. Whoever
you are, this experiment's over.

Morning at last:

see how long frost

remains in the hemlocks' shadow?
Down to breakfast now. I'm starved.

GRAVEYARD MAPLES AFTER SLEET

All night the sleet's black beak pecks
at stones and sills. A solid freeze
arrives with dawn—above the graves
each maple twig is fleshed with ice.
Hold a hand in yours long enough
and the flesh turns to glass.
You stroke a fruit pit, symmetries of bone.

Despair sways like these boughs,
a sorrow so long-lived it becomes
comfort, goose down, skin.
Your corneas are warped glass,
all droop and distortion. Nothing
limber lingers. Daybreak's a shirt
of chain mail. The sky whitens,
congeals to cooling lard.

Above the graves the sleet has heaped
its white grit—the chalk cloud
of names' erasure, the pale flakes
winter's centuries make of tombs.
Above the graves, ice trellises now,
the maple boughs in steady wind
are creaking, a rhythmic rigging
unmoored from all we know.

THE FAILED ROMANTIC SEDUCES A BLUEBERRY BAR;
OR, A CONFESSIONAL POEM

(not the poet, not me)—John Berryman

Oh, I am living on the edge,
allowing myself caffeine and pastry
once a week, double cappuccino
and a blueberry bar at Bollo's coffee shop
where the young sport their pierced nostrils

and grayless goatees. Hurried coffee break,
then my colloquium on confessional poetry.
Sexton juggles gin and sleeping pills,
Plath watches yew limbs hook the moon,
Lowell brushes leaves from family tombs.

Berryman hankers for death and another drink,
Wakoski mourns another man's betrayal,
sinks a knife into pumpkin pie.
And I? I lived high drama once.
Beneath a Radford bar table, thigh

slid against thigh, hand clasped
hand. Let's blame Killian's
for how adultery began, those furtive
spring afternoons. The tulips burnt
like hurricane lamps, like smudge pots.

Powdered grace, dust-motes
swam down the sun-slants.
His husband safely ensconced
at work, at least once a week we met.
A borrowed A-frame in the woods—

Rhine wine, doughnuts, incense, handcuffs,
legs about my waist, moustache sticky
with champagne or clover honey.
A miracle I didn't die of hairballs.
This morning in the gym, still shower-wet

before the mirror, I tried to count
the silver hairs on my chest. Black
spruce needles rimed with first snow.
These cappuccino-buzz afternoons,
all autumnal, guilt has become

a blueberry bar, the rich sin
of sugar and fat. I sit in the sun,
nibbling and sipping, wondering
how love survives betrayal,
how passion remains, decades later,

for those one can never forgive.
How we diminish, thankful for
comfort, unevent, kindness,
sunlight on October-orange maple leaves.
How we mature, tired of romancing pain.

RELIC

Not golden, not bejeweled, nothing like the reliquaries
of Munich's Residenz, Vienna's Hofburg,
those ornate receptacles for the flotsam and jetsam of
    saints.
Only a cardboard box in the storage room
of my father's house in Hinton, West Virginia.
Inside, amidst occult tomes, rests what I retain
of you. The scrawled, seductive letters you sent
after moving with your husband to Massachusetts.
A thin album of photos, a few bottles of German wine
    we emptied.
The leather teddy bear you bought me in State College,
the silver pentagram ring you mailed me from
    Framingham,
a few flirtatious valentines. And—most intimate
    keepsake—
the last thing I asked from you, mere weeks before we
    parted—
a pair of your white jockey shorts.

What did I expect? That something precious could be
    saved?
Your taste, your scent? The mourning dove's dirge?
The way I felt, those larcenous afternoons?
The first pair of underwear you gave me,

M

cloth still moist from the gym, I slipped inside
a Glad bag, hoping to preserve your sweat.
Fanatic's error. The crotch-musk soon turned to folly,
the faint smell of mildew. Sheepish, I asked again.
The second pair? FTL's, tattered a bit. Folded neatly
    still
inside a box there is no reason to open any longer.

These briefs are scentless after fifteen years,
evidence not of beauty but of failure.
Something for my survivors to throw out
after I am over, souvenir meaningless to all
but me. I would like to lie here, say that once,
when I had you naked and bound, the way I loved you
    most,
I gagged you with this very garment, your own sweaty
    shorts,
then wrapped my arms about your hairy chest and,
as I entered you, relished your muffled moans, but

no, that never happened, that was only another
    ecstasy
our hurried time together did not allow,
one of many revelations we never got to share.
You gave me a pair of white jockey shorts,
you gave me what was easy to give,
reserving the rest for another. What I have left of you

is cotton white, stained by none of rapture's sap.
No longer a fabric I press to my face, no longer
a history of musk to breathe deep.
Flesh will never revisit the saints' finger bones.
Scent and warmth will return to this garment
no more than youth will, youth shared for six months,
then squandered apart. White as the heron
picking low tide for scraps, white as the skin

M

of buttocks beneath their fine coating of fur.
White, the waves' unscrolling epitaph.
White, the paper remaining when words run out.

Two

AEOLIAN

In this mode fog is gathering
C minor in walnut dells.

The leaves drop, yellow moisture,
cast off so discourteously.

Amidst New England asters, another
wayfaring stranger shoulders

his delicate dulcimer, strings
loosened so as not to snap

in cold or loneliness. He falls
in love only with all he knows

is leaving soon. The odd thatch
of black hair on the outer flank

of the hand, the small smooth spot on
a chest otherwise pelted: details only

the reverent retain. Aeolian autumn
is stunning the pastures, fingerpicking

the first threat of frost, a fragile dew.

A man in the city stands on a rooftop

in a Sargasso of rooftops; a soldier
in the Sahara reads letters from

West Virginia and squints with salt.
Wayfarers insulate themselves as best

they can, in denim, in leather, in
another generation's scraps, the pieced

salvation of quilts, the memories
of commensal body heat. They move

in minor keys towards hearths
whose fuel they themselves

with straining backs in dream
provide, towards broad beds alone,

towards mulled cider and soup-beans,
a family graveyard, a mountain tune.

LOCRIAN

Where is there to rest?
Not the pasture, where the ground-cherries plumped,

where, in late summer, ironweed pooled.
Not the forest, where the flicker hammered,

where we walked among the emerald,
illicit hand in hand, where we sucked nectar

from nipped honeysuckle blooms. Not the loft
of last century's barn, where hay scratched our cheeks

as we lay through the rain, storm strumming
corrugated tin, sipping moonshine from a flask,

beard to beard, post-seminal drowse. Not
the farmhouse porch, or wedding-ring quilt, or the
    pantry full

of canned peaches, corn relish, half-runners.
You left long ago, for another life,

and tonight I am landless, driving these backroads
    drunk,
snow swirling in the headlights, and what we owned

M

is gone.

Now strangers yank our oaks from the earth.
Tree roots sprawl against the sky. They gasp like
    landed trout,

stacked shoulder to shoulder, bier-burnt. It is a
    blessing now, how
you are not here, how you do not see machines break
    the moss-

stained stones, stain the streams with vermilion,
    tangerine, puce,
bury the water deep. My grandfather's pasture is a
    bowl

of shattered shale, the maple grove a heap of boulders,
a clatter of coal trucks. The well is dry, the farmhouse
    flattened,

the cornfield a great beast's dung-heap, where it
    scratches up
dust and hides its waste. There is only the graveyard
    left,

where, each Memorial Day, we trimmed the spruce
    boughs
and the weeds about the graves, then lay together,
    naked

inside May, inside young grass and red maple shade.
Once I hoped we might have ended here, this fret
    where,

after unrelenting dissonance, a callused forefinger
    slides

into peace, into resolution. Ferrell Ridge, last tooth left

in a shattered mouth. Headstone bearing one name,
not two. I lean against it, pretending it is a mighty tree.

I sip from the pewter flask you bought me in Scotland.
In Celtic swirls, two warriors share a cup.

Tomorrow the blasting and digging will begin again,
rocks fall from the sky, hills upend themselves, but
    tonight

it is silent enough to hear the chimes of frost, the slow
    way
ice marries my moustache. I take another swig. I
    cannot feel my toes.

Tonight I will trace the stars, stroke the few last trees.
Someone must stay to console the dead, name the
    mountains that are gone.

IONIAN

June. Chicory's sapphire, grassy thighs, boys down by
the reservoir, drinking cheap wine and sprawling half-
 naked
on car hoods, soaking in the sun, the wrinkles to
 come.

Ionian is the first tuning, the easiest, major chords of
 college days,
the years before complexity, before deaths line up
like onyx abacus beads. The Greek restaurant on
 Route 19,

long gone, where my mother gave me the larger share
of baklava, and, like most sons, I met generosity
not with gratitude but growing entitlement. Ionia in
 Asia Minor,

the library of Ephesus, apple tea, the long bodiless
 nights with Kevin,
every night retsina, ouzo, and tentacles. He was not
 Patroclus,
I was not Achilles, and the Greeks of Thessaloniki
 lived not

in temples but in concrete ant-hills, the roofs bristling

M

with antennae.
Ionian in Sunnyside, the first dulcimer I strummed,
    hemlocks glistening
the windows with green, and Wayne from Michigan—
    we always competed

who could hug whom the hardest—sitting on Cin's
    couch,
teaching us "A Case of You," and, later, in white jockey
    shorts,
sleeping on the couch, the fur on his chest, his hard
    nipples,

his beard my fear did not stroke. That barn on the
    Mileground,
half-heated craft fair, Cin and Cindy and I sitting on
    hay bales
by the pot-bellied stove, playing "Carey" and growing
    warmer

on mugs of spiced cider and rum. "The Rose" at the
    last coffeehouse
in Morgantown, West Virginia, The Last Resort,
    where we gobbled
between sets blueberry crepes with whipped cream,
    crepes

so exotic and cosmopolitan to this country boy.
    "Amazing Grace,"
my grandmother's knotty hands on the upright, after
    the green beans
with ham bone, after the pecan pie—and who will
    love me like that again?

"Will Ye No Come Back Again" and "Skye Boat Song"—
    I remember

M

the thistles of Glencoe, and Graham shaking out the Drambuie-
amber of his ponytail, over pints offering me hand-rolled cigarettes, or

striding proudly from that Edinburgh changing room in his new
blue-and-green Campbell kilt, the summer that ethics coated my tongue
and hands with bark. An animal, paralyzed, might as well be tree or stone.

"Loch Lomond" I strum this morning, remembering men and kin I will never meet again.
Ionian is the mode of should-be, where desire is free to act, desire finds itself returned.
I was young then. The sun was major and midsummer. The family was complete.

DORIAN

Hopelessly medieval. I strum "Scarborough Fair" and
 wish
I were there to guard Edward the Second from his
 enemies.
Brainpans would cleave, neat and satisfying, like fish
November splits, spilling milkweed seeds out along
 the breeze.

Music the starry white of virgin's bower, perfumed
 heat dying
at dusk. Mists nudge the line of pines behind the
 farmhouse,
the pickup's window thickens with ghosts. Gauzy
September steps in. A hurry about the farmers'
 market,

squirrels gathering provender for the cold to come.
The red ventricles of peppers, the purple
Middle Eastern mirrors of eggplant, smell of vinegar
and garlic in the kitchen. Fruit flies swarm over

compost, the fireflies are done. In the song, black was
the color of my true love's hair. Brown, I think, but
that remains to be seen. A mode not minor, but
 incomplete.

ᛗ

The modalities of late summer, the mourning of
 crickets,

black armor heaped up in dewfall. The man in the
 corn
strips off his shirt, shakes pollen from his beard.
 Smiling,
he lifts his fists, scatters golden seed across the earth.
Wind rustles the stalks, and the sun's gleam is
 weariness,

sweat. Soon enough he will bow his head, cross thick
 wrists
behind his back. He will be ready for the sword then,
 ready
for the binding, ready to wrap his body's pelt-warmth
about mine and sleep together in the cave's long cold.

PHRYGIAN

Hurricane's remnants on the tin roof all night,
Frances, my mother's middle name. Irish Breakfast tea,
and the rain continues hard all morning, summer's
last green surrounding this old house like wet
    malachite.
I skip the gym, I strum this spruce-and-mahogany box

on my lap, and mourning moves through the blue urn
of ashes on my father's mantel, and my father's island,
where cliffs are unscalable, and what beaches there are
flower with blue-gray barbed wire, and on to great
    earth-
maimings and meadow-murders south of Charleston,

West Virginia, coal barges on the Kanawha, and snow-
    spotted
coal stealing past Hinton in car after car. This melody
    lives far
from Phrygia, far from the long-extinct tongues of
    Asia Minor.
It winds instead through Ireland's black pudding and
    gooseberry jam,
the scent of peat-smoke so like the armpits of a lover
    I had

M

just lost, and the stone farmhouses crumbling, not as fast
as coal camps, but collapsing nonetheless. Finally the forefinger
slides along D minor and settles on the man I might have been,
born not to liberals, free-thinkers, but to others, in Ballard, Meadow Bridge,
Danese, in Cashmere, Stanaford, Union. Here are the cherub

met at the Gay March on Washington, the one banned from Williamson's
public pool when the town found out he was positive, and Arthur Warren,
run over repeatedly near Fairmont, and Justen, punched in the face
in his high school's halls, forced to leave Boone County. This mode is in them,
my lonely brothers, the small-town men without men. They sleep in their secret,

their useless tenderness, in the shadow of steeples, in the thick country dark.
They learn to cherish Greek cookbooks, Krispy Kreme, fried green tomatoes,
photos of Tim McGraw taped to the refrigerator door. Rain on tin roofs,
new flannel sheets, self-reliant flesh in the fist. Books and videos:
Achilles and Patroclus, Hephaestion and Alexander, Colin and Brad.

Phrygian is this minor fact, the way a simple percentage hems us in, the way
a sea-born storm exhausts itself, fierce and alone. In

M

    this morning's mountains,
a man mirrors what he loves. I see his black beard and
    beer gut, his wife-beater
and boots, his camo pants. He steers a 4x4 through
    the lashing rockabilly rains,
heading to town to buy bourbon, sorghum, acorn
    squash seeds, pinto beans.

LYDIAN

It all moves so easily,
like ivy up the cabin wall,
like the tiny stars of wind-
borne seeds, fragile as ardor.
This is the dream of the countryside,
Appalachian Arcadia, where

the fingers, the tongue,
the mossy body step into
completion. Here, everywhere
we stand we are satisfied.
Big breakfasts—buckwheat cakes
and sausage—then long afternoons

of labor leading to welcome
freedom from need. In this music,
the ideal's still intact, the day's
a gleaming vase for gladioli,
a bowl brimming with okra,
hot peppers, ripe ears of corn.

Men are made of summer.
Stripped to the waist, comrades
sweat side by side in the hayfields,
swilling jars of well water,

heaving the scratchy bales
like golden loaves of bread

from field to truck to loft,
then bathing in streams, drowsing in warm
grass, young skin. Home's the scent
of baking biscuits, jars of honey.
The evening star rises over lavender lines
of hills, a music full of yearning,

a yearning so easily resolved.
No food stamps, draglines, coal trucks.
No evangelism, oxycontin, or trailer-fires.
Chords instead, green-gold as new maple leaves,
as perfect as dream and pastoral insist
these innocent mountains might have been.

MIXOLYDIAN

The octaves are endless, beyond
our capacity for hearing. The bass string
sounds middle C, and echoes of that descend,
through the floorboards and the cellar of the house
and into autumn's dirt, through layers of humus,
history's rich decay, the ribcage of sandstone, and on
    into
liquid crimson, the fire we would enter in the heart of
    the earth.

The melody strings shiver even untouched,
sympathetic vibrations, like responding to like,
as below, so above, one note calling on another,
its heavenly twin. These echoes rise, C above middle
    C,
and on up the scale, outstripping our sense, bounding
    over
the hurdle of the skull, through maple-burn beginning
    in
the treetops, and so through cirrus and ozone and
    into

the company of myth, those hearth-embers some
    hand
shaped like ours has scattered about the

compassionate sky.
This chord is open, brief, complete. Inside it, the
    Queen Anne's lace,
dying, invites Orion. Cathedrals mimic emerald naves
    within
the green pepper. Rain-wet corn, inside its papery
    swaddle,
swells tonight in the light of a full moon, and the
    moon sings
to itself in the waters of the farm pond. Our bodies
    are both

bass and treble. We sit in sunlight, one smile evoking
    another.
Today, tomorrow, next year or life, we might touch.
    Now that desire
has become not need but want, not subsistence but
    largesse, I will live
with fancy for a while, studying how the sky mirrors
    your skin and mine.
In our torsos, muscles move like magma. After labor,
    sweat's the scent of moss.
In the grave-mound's core, we strike life from flint.
    Kindling sparks, flames,
spring's first coltsfoot. Over broken mountains, the
    solstice sunrise answers.

THREE

SEPTEMBER SUNLIGHT

The sky opens this morning
like a dayflower. Sapphire
petals, with mica flecks,
the sun a golden stamen.

In classrooms across campus,
teachers stop speaking,
students stop speaking,
watch the televisions instead.

Midafternoon, classes cancelled,
at loose ends I head down the hill
for coffee. Beech nuts pop beneath my boots,
somewhere a woodpecker's drumming.

By now the broad bed, where
three weeks ago my lover and I slept,
in a hotel room overlooking the Hudson,
has joined the rest in ruin.

Before the coffee shop, a scruffy-bearded boy
I know sits bare-chested in the sun,
and soon I join him. We sip our coffees
silently, two whom evil has not chosen,

M

watching wind shuttle leaves
down the street, thinking of the dead
so far from here. He's naked
save for cut-off denim shorts, showing off,

in these last warm days, a body still young.
The fur on his chest and thighs is golden,
the skin of his shoulders lacquered with sun.
I smell armpit musk, spicy as cumin.

The grass is thin on what will be my gravesite,
like fine hair on these wrinkled hands.
About our feet the locust leaves, dull topaz,
smoulder like scattered finger bones, too many to
    count.

September sunlight includes it all: the boy's
fine muscles, these restless leaves, the stink of fuel,
that empty space where towers of steel used to stand.
Above the smoke, the sun's eye does not blink.

SEPTEMBER MORNING FOG

I'm halfway down Flat Top Mountain
when it washes in, this pallid sea of fog,

swallowing the goldenrod, the swallowtails,
robbing color from the pastures, the rainbowed

roadcuts, forcing all into the same gray hue.
Even now, men pick through the ruined towers, trying to count

the dead. How patient grief can be, keeping its distance
for years before moving in again. No one is spared.

All those lost, all those with everything to lose,
now it is our turn to drive through this daylight darkness.

What can we do but be patient ourselves,
patient as sorrow has been?

It is the nature of fog to lift,
and though we know it will come again,

for a time there is this: the sky of September,

blue as a morning glory, unstained by tarry smoke.

Only here and there, defiant against that blue,
the fading white signature of a jet trail.

SUGAR MAPLES IN OCTOBER

(for Mark Bingham; died September 11, 2001)

Within October's cathedral,
    the woods' gray naves and colonnades,
sugar maples are burning.
    Brief stained glass,
chemical bonfires of carotene.
    Each leaf before its end
is allowed such glory, before nights
    of November rain
shatter the gothic glass,
    before shards of orange
and red skitter down the street,
    heap against curbsides
to rot in ashy aftermath.
    You were the sort of man,
I'm guessing,
    I would love to have glimpsed
in the locker room.
    Even now, magazine photos
of your face graft
    onto those memories
of strangers' bodies
    I've desired from a distance.
I see you drying off
    after the shower,
running a lucky towel

M

    along those rugby shoulders,
along those lightly furred
    athlete's pecs.
Lust is personal, not ideological,
    and the only
hatred I understand
    is personal as well.
Now you're toweling off, now
    lying warm and naked
atop me in this chilly
    autumn apartment,
amorous beneath flannel sheets,
    as mid-morning sunlight streaks
a pile of textbooks,
    a sugar pumpkin's burnt orange.
No, this fantasy's
    too smeared with the impossible.
What's clearer is the way
    history happened,
even the moments no one alive
    is left to describe.
What I want is
    to watch you use
those big muscles your lovers
    ran their reverence along,
the muscles that hefted
    barbells, that drove in
the goal. I want to see you
    from your seat near the cockpit
rise, slam that hijacker
    against the side of the plane,
drive the coward's plastic knife
    into his ideological guts.
This is personal:
    to take from you, from me,
the way maples immolate

M

 October, the way men's bodies
arch beneath our fingers.
 Most of us are spared
the hero's last ecstasy,
  the martyr's farewell flame.
To seize an enemy
  who has engineered your certain death,
to wrap your fingers
  around his throat
and squeeze, your body bigger
  than his, your strength greater.
Watch the panic rise
  in his eyes, bear down
on his thrashing, watch the light
  fade like floodwaters,
the breath fly off
  leaf by maple leaf,
as you take all that ambitious evil
  with you into the mud.

BLACK WINDOWS

The word is "potterracking,"
odd Appalachian term,
describing the racket guinea hens make,
or, in this case, a loud gabble-
gaggle of businesswomen
who will not shut up though it's
the last hour before dawn and
everyone else on the plane
is trying to sleep. What fascinates me

is how, mannerless, they seem to live
the narcissistic fantasy I can only dream—
that the planet is theirs alone, that others
exist only as audience, as prop.
How fine it must be to know
everything you say is of interest to everybody.
How excellent to have a mouth that inexhaustible
in a world where, really, there is less and less
of importance to say. More and more,

it is silence I choose, turning towards
black windows in which the mountains,
the last of the night, shift by beneath me.
First, the lights of Charleston, West Virginia,
curving along the Kanawha. Then, as we fly

south towards Charlotte, hills of the coalfields,
and one great gray flatness where machines
have torn off the mountaintop to reach the last
of the coal. The blood of hills is acid, gray
or orange, staining the creek-beds. How often,

within each minute, is someone conceived,
does someone give birth? Down the aisle,
the potterracking mounts, voice layered on voice,
strata of shrieks. Between the mountains,
lights slither along the valleys, promising
to improve paradise, gleaming like phosphorescent
snail trails, radioactive spoor. The mountains
    themselves,
the mountains that remain, are too steep
for trailer park, automobile dealership, mall.
This distant from dawn, unpeopled,
they are black arching against black.
It is only darkness that gives me hope.

ℳ

4x4

1.
A man sits alone in a house surrounded by snow,
surrounded by mountains. He drinks Irish whiskey,
he reads Ovid, bakes bread, listens to Puccini. I cannot tell
whether the man is my father or myself.
I seem to have borrowed every gesture I own.

2.
Every Southerner's worst fear.
I have outstayed my welcome,
and in my father's house at that.
When I reach for the warrior
I have trained so long, the thickness
of a forearm swinging a sword,
I find only a child, useless, in tears, and all
those trophies and triumphs I brought
have made no difference, winged seeds
of the sugar maple skittering across asphalt.

Words, so. To have words.
To stare at his rage, at my grizzled beard
in the weeping mirror. Where is manhood
in the face of him, in the face of God,
who so fearfully loves and guards his solitude?

ℳ

The morning I was born, something stellar knew
it would all coincide, this last weekend of July:

My sister is pregnant, I have adopted
a kitten off the streets, I have thrown
the second Manhattan in the sink.
There is little to pack, but before I leave,
I pluck the maraschino cherry from the drain,
just as my father would, flip it into compost
where it will not be wasted. The kitten cries
only a little in his box as we crest Sandstone Mountain
in the ten-year-old 4x4 Toyota Tacoma I bought off
Daddy last winter. $7,000 for this assurance:
now I can go anywhere, into and out of snow.

3.

By the time the kitten and I reach the Kanawha Valley,
I am sober, it approaches midnight, on the radio
Tim McGraw, the most beautiful man in the world,
is singing his new hit, "Live Like You Were Dying."
Behind the chords, he's mourning his father's early
    death.
Baseball star, cancer patient. The son strokes his
    father's hand,
his own goatee, tips the brim of his hat over his face.
Soon both of them will be eclipsed by white light,
devoured. Soon my father will be eighty-four.
Soon my partner John will welcome me home.

4.

Cinder blocks, bags of cat litter or sand.
Nothing worked. The ass-end of every
rear-wheel-drive pickup I owned shimmied
and bucked like erotic dancers, queens in heat,
on rain-wet pavement, on slush or the slightest

M

snow. Forty-five, and I call my father Daddy,
as Southern men will. Daddy, those fears are behind me
now, that sick stomach-lurch as the truck slides crab-wise
sideways and into a ditch. Women joke, but they are right:
there is phallic confidence in it, shifting the stick
into four-wheel-drive and tearing out of my snow-heaped
unshoveled driveway, or heading up that rut-rough slope
above the Roanoke River to drink wine with mountaintop
buddies, knowing I will get where I want, over even
that most frightful of bitches, Flat Top Mountain, where
frost lingers and the blizzards hold court.
I will call them gifts, though they came with a price,
the ways you taught me to need no one, to love no one,
to negotiate the sleet and move away from you.

5.

Wind thunders the tin roof tonight.
Bolognese sauce simmers on the stove.

I want music while I cook, soundtrack to
The Return of the King up loud, and

Isle of Jura single malt to sip till
John gets here from West Virginia.

For a long time I watch the way wind moves
limbs of the white oak, shakes

∽

snow from limbs of spruce. Soughing, no doubt,
a word my father taught me. The night is purple

in ruts my truck wheels have cut into white.
Shadow at the bottom of shadow, shadow of

a shadow. Embrace later, Manhattans, the grating
of cheese, Netflix, flannel sheets, the holding and then

the falling apart, a separate sleep. Love, it is my
    pedigree, to love
the loneliness near dawn, two men sleeping with
    warm space

between. 4x4, the Sphinx's riddle. We fall from
    adulthood,
precarious verticality, we crawl away on hands and
    knees.

WRITERS' TOUR OF KAYFORD MOUNTAIN
—OCTOBER 16, 2006

(for Edwina Pendarvis and Katie Fallon)

Today's quiet is arranged for us, the tourists of
    evisceration.
None of the usual dynamite, none of the usual

draglines gnawing innards like hagfish or lamprey.
It's an abeyance too large to fill

with words, though I try, naming plants
growing still in the face of blasphemy, mere

inches from the edge. I hug Eddy,
whisper *lamb's quarter, lady's thumb,*

motherfuckers, motherfuckers.
In what was heart and now is hole, air mounts

and hardens, dust swirls and settles, the felled
trees smoulder, a useless fuel. *Wild*

strawberry, dewberry, pokeweed. Crows circle
where the planet's darkness once was

dense, is now dispersed, in the emptiness left inside
when entrails are uncoiled and minced into bits.

Far below, a few trucks grumble with inertia,
sun shudders in the pit's black pools,

on the shattered shale. Here the forest ends,
the long drop begins. Here cedar waxwings

turn back. *Sumac's red, sugar maple's burn.*
Our weakness disappoints the dead. Here,

in the shiver of lavender asters, their faces appear,
their mute lips move. Glowering, they dissolve.

GREG'S PARTY

Deployment's the odd word
on the e-mail invite. Here is
this tiny house in Pulaski,
this small sweet handsome man
heading for some damned camp,
then Kuwait or Afghanistan.
Here are gin and tonics,
canapés, some brave glasses
of champagne, the much-
needed buzz. Here I am
annoyed when the hot cream
of Crab Rangoon spits over
my silk shirt. Outside,
on the porch, the day-
lilies burn, the festive
bubble machine, in perfect
silence, exudes one sphere
after another, each a wet
skin the sheen of rainbow.
The breeze strays them,
their summer ranks spread,
they take their turns,
they glitter, they burst.

THREE CROSSES

(for Cynthia Burack)

Isn't the ironweed enough?
And the hemlock needles edged with frost,
as if a castle's crenellations were carved from crystal?

To remind us of God's glory,
he said, and squandered a fortune on crosses,
trios blue and gold, making Calvary common as the
    next pasture,

the next interstate curve.
Isn't the Storm Moon enough, white pine boughs
shaking off snow? Crocus resurrection, purple and
    gold?

This is what you do,
with your fat book of black and gold,
your love of mirrors, your stained-glass abbatoirs.

He sagged on that prairie
fence for hours. She ran away from home.
His body was found in a toilet. She hung herself in the
    barn.

This is what you do,
your prayers muttered in the voter's booth,

M

your certainty that a soiled world is soon due to end
>with you.

~

Evil sees evil
everywhere. And so the streams run
orange, mountaintops peel off like scabs, red spruce
>needles

dissolve beneath sulfuric drizzle.
Evil only loves its own reflection, in broken
glass, in slurry puddles. Evil only loves what is eternal.

~

What I want's a savior
in my sheets, brief as that bliss might be.
Brown eyes, brown goatee, thunderheads of body hair.

Some scruffy Christ
roped down, ball-gagged and melodic, eager as any
>sacrifice
to be eaten. What I want's a mountain landscape
>without a wound.

What I want's the skill
to break the jaw of vicious piety, the strength
to rescue what I love. What I want's a chainsaw on
>Easter Sunday,

and a heap of broken crosses
for the Beltane bonfire. My new world's the ring-
>dance,
the blaze, wine scented with woodruff, benediction of
>maple leaves.

ALAN TURING MEMORIAL — MANCHESTER

(IN MEMORY OF ALAN TURING, 1912-1954)

(for Angelia Wilson and Cynthia Burack)

This is how we meet, in a garden,
not the original one, of course, but
Sackville Gardens, one of the smaller,
more contemporary simulacra
of which the English are masters, here
among piebald patches of crocus, blue,
yellow, and white, here where the pink
of the March-mad cherry ruffles and fans—
a snow-chime if color might bleed sound,
tintinnabulations, that Latinate treasure—
here near the canal, the soothing rush
and foam of water falling, near spangled
gay bars, young men cruising, near
the Beacon of Hope, that silver spiral
commemorating all those who suffer
from AIDS (worm new come to English
Eden), here we meet near midnight,
as I escort two lesbian friends home
after several pints of those British beers
and ciders I so rarely enjoy back home
in Appalachia, they and I crossing
the park in the dark, and I, paranoid
country boy in a foreign city, spying
a man sitting motionless on a bench—
perhaps, who knows? someone dangerous—

M

some gay basher who's chosen the wrong
queers to fuck with, but no, it's you,
I recognize the name on the plaque,
I know why you sit here in the dark, alone,
clutching your apple, *father of computer science,
victim of prejudice,* so many decades dead.

How are queers like West Virginians? asks the queer
West Virginian. Ha, ha, so might begin an excellent
gay joke or hillbilly jest. Because we're all sick of
being mocked, and so we gather the names of fame
about us, those who prove how fine we might become.
So I knew you before I sat beside you in the dark,
    knew
how you helped save England by cracking Nazi codes,
how soon thereafter your ingrate country turned on
    you,
hero suddenly criminal, charged with gross indecency,
the very same law that sentenced Oscar Wilde
to hard labor two years, breaking himself on rocks.
Science gave you another option; the chemistry
you cherished saved you for another fate.

Jail or chemical castration? Testosterone's
the god we love—the hard penis, the armpit
musk, the hair across chest and belly, in
the crack of the ass, semen strung like
sticky constellations across a lover's beard.
What did estrogen injections erase?
Did your desire for men dwindle, grass
burnt brown in summer heat, wild mess
of brambles pruned down to nothing?
Did you shave less often, less often
touch yourself? Did your breasts plump
and droop? Did acid corrode the muscled

statues, shutter your sight? Did beauty
burn down to stumps and char, fire pit
chewing up your useless lips and fingers?

Manchester's Gay Village, the largest in Europe,
if only you could see it now, right across Rochdale Canal
from your quiet, crocus-studded garden. Alan, twinks
are on the twilight prowl, in their tight clothes and breathless
gleaming, eager to sit on someone's lap. Nightfall, pinprick
lights of blue gleam like hairnet sapphires in trees lining
the water. It's a drizzly North-of-England evening,
I'm drinking Strongbow at Taurus, bulky bear in denim,
brown leather, boots, and *Butch Built* baseball cap,
sitting beside a straight cross-dresser in mink coat, rose
quartz jewelry, Chinese gown, beside Angie and Cindy,
butt-kicker academic dykes showing me the town.
It's a blustery North-of-England afternoon, and I'm
gobbling steak and ale pie in Via's snug window seat,
among the dark wood of disassembled Gothic churches,
watching rain claw the glass with silver, wind tip table
umbrellas into the canal, tattooed leather studs stride by.
I'm buying porn at Clone Zone, hairy bearded cowboys
bobbing on cocks or getting it up the ass; I'm cruising
for a submissive, goateed cub I can bind and gag and ravish,
at least in dream. Alan, it's a new world on Canal Street

ᛖ

(remove the C and S, and what you get's *Anal Treet*).
Long gone, it seems, that ignorant decade in which
    you died.

~

I'm researching you on my Apple
MacBook Pro, trim descendant of the slow
and bulky first computers you helped invent,
when up comes e-mail, a local middle-school
teacher has been fired once the fucking
Baptist minister/principal found out
said teacher was gay and thus a fierce
threat to children, this news the same
week that two kids are gay-bashed on
the campus of UVA, this news the same
week a West Virginia high-school
senior's asking the board of education
to stop anti-gay bullying in Kanawha County,
this not long after a kid in Massachusetts,
eleven years old, weary of enduring
gay slurs in grade school, hangs himself.
Of the world's streets, Canal's one of very few
where, for men like us, the world is safely new.

~

Angie's arranged the reading: "Poetry and Prose
of an Appalachian Leather Bear." The audience is small,
like most of mine, authors not having much draw
when faced with the stiff competition of slick and hip
baby bands, street-cruising, text-messaging, video
    games.
Still, I call on you, hoping you will leave your eternal
garden of cherry blossoms and crocuses, cross
the splashing canal, settle in a corner of this lounge
beneath Taurus Bar and Grill, where I speak so frankly
of desires you had to hide in a vicious age that turned
to poison all that is fruitful, juicy, sweet. I want you

ℳ

and your fellows, those terrified, intimidated
 generations,
to hear and see and savor all this. Watch: my little
 Jesus
shakes out his Drambuie-amber hair and drops his
 towel.
Watch: my lover with his thick-muscled, thick-furred
 pecs
is chewing a jockstrap moist as I lap Lindisfarne mead
from his groin. He bucks and moans, wet-eyed when
I ease off the nipple clamps and jack him slowly with
 my fist.
I will speak again and again of what men like you
 could not.

It's in the smell of cherry twigs, sweet
and bitter, acrid almond, and in wilted
black cherry leaves that kill the browsing
heifer. It's in apple seeds and cherry pits.
How did you do it, poison the apple?
Hypodermic needle? Simple steeping?
I am no scientist, but you were, you knew
what you were about, taking inside
not the flesh of men but cyanide,
leaving behind the shame, the estrogen
treatments, the amputated career.
Apple of the golden Strongbow cider
pints I sip on *Anal Treet*, reddened buttocks
of a muffled bound-down boy marked by
sadist's teeth, plump apple of the wisdom
tree, of "Snow White," your favorite fairy tale,
apple plump and bitten on my laptop lid,
found half-eaten by your body, by your bed.

We might have done as you did. You would do

M

as we do now, given what this time and place allow,
men kissing and holding hands, dancing in honest
daylight, in crocus-spring, along Rochdale Canal.
I need to tell you what's possible, how what's grim
can be revised. The prince eats the poisoned apple,
true, just as you chose to do. He lies in state, skin
as white as apple flesh, as snowy moor, as Pennine
mist, lips as red as blood, beard as black as ebony.
He sleeps for centuries, statue in a coffin made of ice.
What wakes him? History? A cleft in the clouds,
sunlight upon his lips, his brow? The chilly trickle
of water unbound, reviving? A lover's kiss, a lover's
hard fist pounding his chest? At last he heaves up
the smoky chunks of poison, the hard black tears
of apple seeds. He finds himself slumped naked
in garden grass, in the cherries' wind-strewn petals,
in runnels of wind ruffling black hair upon his breast.
Body and sense seep back slowly after such a tomb,
after such an icy sleep. He will lie here awhile, panting
in the sun, gathering his drowsy strength, stroking
warmth into his long-numb skin, till all the bliss
he's missed grips his hand and pulls him to his feet.

VIRGINIA FANTASIA

Spring morning in Blacksburg, Virginia:
hedge of blooming lilacs, golden drift
of white-oak pollen, and this listserv note

announcing that the General Assembly
of this great state, state of Washington and Jefferson,
state where I was born, has just passed

the Marriage Affirmation Act, which prohibits
civil unions and outlaws "any partnership,
contract or other arrangements that purport

to provide the benefits of marriage."
I smash a coffee cup, call my sister for legal advice,
ask about the complications of changing

state citizenship, but West Virginia,
it turns out, is much the same on this score.
11 am—Creative Writing/Poetry:

I read my students Mark Doty's poem
"Charlie Howard's Descent," in which hoodlums
throw a young gay man off a bridge to his death.

In between the first class and the second,

in the men's bathroom, second floor of McBryde Hall,
I'm washing my hands when I see, in the mirror over
    the sink,

FUCK YOU FAGGOTS, large black letters
inked into the wall of a toilet stall. Afternoon's end,
a guest lecture in "The Appalachian Family and its
    Environment,"

I'm talking about mountain cooking—ramps, creecy
    greens,
brown beans and cornbread, the foods I grew up on,
the foods that make me feel safe and at home

in these hills—I'm wondering what the members
of the General Assembly of the Commonwealth
of Virginia will be enjoying for dinner tonight.

Walking back to my office, I pass young men
playing basketball: pale, shirtless, sweating,
remote. I press my face, my yearning,

into the pink blossoms of an apple tree
and think of King Arthur, wounded, floating off
to paradise, the Isle of Apples, where strife's

a stranger and every appetite's answered.
Dinner with friends, a visiting writer's reading,
then home, tired, to sip single malt,

grade a few student journals. In bed by ten.
Tomorrow, the drive up to Charleston,
another weekend with John, but

tonight alone, loving the solitude and silence,
far from those I love and those I hate.

Night breeze wafts the curtains in. I strip,

light a candle, take from its wall-mount
Aragorn's elven hunting knife, curved
scimitar engraved with elvish, *Foe*

of Morgoth's Realm. For a minute I stand
before the mirror naked, studying
the salt-and-pepper goatee, hard-won muscles,

tribal tattoos. What I loathe most
is any constriction that limits
what this body might choose.

What I love is the world reimagined, revised.
I stretch out on the bed, cold blade sleeping
in the silver hair between my pecs. I run my fingers

over the etched elvish, the sharp edge, rub the band
of gold about my ring finger, and close my eyes.
I fondle these irreconcilables side by side:

wedding among Turkey Spur's blooming
rhododendrons, John in his conductor's tuxedo,
I in my Maclaine of Lochbuie kilt, dirk at my side,

and Aragorn atop me now, smiling in the candlelight,
lean and hairy, his long hair falling
over my face, his beard brushing my lips,

and every man I have ever wanted, on the street,
in the bars or in the gyms, an eternity of touch,
endlessly various, perpetuities of sweat and
    candlelight,

and a farmhouse with a porch, in the lap of the

M

    mountains,
John's flower beds, maples burnt-orange with autumn,
biscuits and gravy, slate trivets and canning jars,

and this knife brought down again and again,
the last No silenced, a heap of heads, the ravens'
    eyeball-feast.
I want a warrior's well-deserved rest, drowsing by

the hall's hearth-fire, bare shoulder to shoulder, beard
married to beard, darkness welded to light, golden
quaichs of Drambuie or mead, toasting the end of our
    enemies.

TULIP TREES, VIRGINIA TECH

These leaves, they were here
as I was not, that April day
of hard wind, sunlight mixed
with hail. They were small
then, unfolding slow their new
green-gold, Frost's *hardest hue
to hold,* fingers once knotted
in prayer opening and lifting
toward coming summer's light.
Tonight, in the glow of street-
lamps, they are aging, mottled
orange and brown, the rotting
chlorophyll of 2007. Placards
nailed to the doors of Norris Hall
are orange too, and the few lights
glowing inside well-mopped
classrooms. I stride by cursing
one I never met, imagining
eternities of strappado,
God's glowing grindstones,
keen-edged eviscerations.
Two blonde girls pass my dark
and muttering bristle by.
One nuzzles her cell phone,
whispering low. One whistles

and flits through humming
streetlamps' shrouds of light,
through the crunch of leaves
September's chosen first to fall.

SHEATH

What blessed sheath is this,
to know none of those who died?

Sheath of the milkweed, sheath
of green-gold the tulip tree leaves split like votive
    smoke.

Sheath of the cicada, its claws of dirty glass left
clinging to tree bark, emptiness and a cleft back the
    soul's only evidence.

Six months later, carefully timed,
there are candles, there are lawsuits,

as if burning wax or financial recompense could ever
    answer
accident, make of madness

an etiology one could comprehend,
clutch in the palm, apotropaic as buckeye

or rabbit's foot. I'm rereading
Marcus Aurelius, and he seems to be trying

to convince himself that all he and we suffer

M

is weakness. The strong, it seems, detach.

This is not helpful. Now there are peepholes
in classroom doors, complex locks, there are 32

poles bearing the flags of victim nations
erected before the Baptist church. In strong

or even moderate wind, there's a rattling, rattling,
as if the flags were cursing or confabulating. I more
    than understand

viciousness justifiably directed. I have a hit list
a mile long I dream of working down were I
    diagnosed with six months to live.

Like Raskolnikov, I might be fooling myself, but
my guess is that some killing would find me rapturous,

the rush of reservoir waters undammed at last,
a great milky load after being cruelly edged for hours.

Sheath of the pig-fucker's handgun, sheath of the
    hunting knife
beneath my pickup seat, sheath of the army knife
    beside my bed.

Insanity's imbedded in the random, we're in
    agreement there?
Agreed I drink too much. I contemplate how much
    human happiness

a few precognitive abortions might provide. The
    drought's
gone on so long the governor's talking disaster area.

At night, someone keeps tugging the blankets off me. Gin keeps me up. I cannot sleep till I hear my husband snore.

FEASTING IN THE AFTERMATH

The lesson's simple. We need reminding, the world
    kindly reminds us
again and again. Stepping over home's threshold, into
    routine, murmur
Take nothing for granted, murmur *I might not have
come back to this.*

Wrong day, wrong building for dying. Teaching on
    Tuesdays, not Mondays,
not in Norris Hall but in McBryde. *No one knows the
day and hour,*
the preachers are wont to mutter, the mountain
    fatalists whose forbears

fetched predestination's pall from the Lowlands and
    the Borders.
His eye is on the sparrow? Indeed? Distracted by birds
    that day?
Busy summoning omens? The weird April flurries,
    wind's hard gnaw

blackening new buds, scattering Bradford pear
    blossoms, making way
for carnage. *Mysterious ways,* no more
    comprehensible than constellations

are countable. In the media-sorry aftermath, drive
past late April's greening

pastures, the mindlessness of cattle, brooks lined with
box elder and willow.
Come home to swarming cats, a spouse who's cooked
comfort food all day.
Martinis, pita bread, spinach and artichoke dip. Fried
chicken, coleslaw,

macaroni and cheese baked golden-brown, a fat slice
of coconut cake.
Every celebration's desperate. In bed together, rub his
furry belly,
solid still, still warm. *Years yet,* demands the body,
years yet, years yet.

SUNDAY MORNING BISCUITS

I beat you to death last night,
slamming your head into brick
again, again, again, again—
it took bear-brawn, passion,
and patience—but I persisted
till the longed-for, dreamed-after
brain pan split like balsa wood,
like milkweed pods releasing
gray-silk November seeds.
Figurative language is a pretty
gloss, isn't it, smoothing
over the spill of cerebral
convolutions. The Latinate
elegantly sidesteps as well,
sidesteps the sweet, the illegal,
the grim ecstasies of what
few would ever admit:
what delight it would be
to bash what's hated into
oozing pieces, steaming chunks,
to match destruction with
destruction. Simpler
diction is more satisfying,
more apt to cause a cringe.
This morning, white, white

M

are the flour, the baking powder,
the buttermilk I mix and knead,
using would-be murderer's
hands to bake biscuits for
husband and friends, biscuits
to top with butter and jam,
mayonnaise and tomatoes,
gravy with Jimmy Dean sausage
and a bit of onion. I remember
when I first fell in love with
demolition: age twenty-one,
tearing down a wall my father
needed removing. I drank
bourbon and beer, listened
to the Mountaineers, took
my father's crowbar to nail, plaster,
wood. Construction took skill,
and back then I had none of that,
but destruction, God, so easy, so
thrilling, making empty
space autumn sun could
stab through. We had
that delight in common,
I suppose, though the reported
expression of your face amid
the slaughter suggests numb
duty more than delight.
You robbed our rage of
recompense. I will get back
to your twitching corpse
tonight. Now I wrap
hot biscuits in a tea towel,
call the boys in to breakfast.
Later, deadheading the day
lilies, kneading seeds into earth's
rich black, I will daydream

M

you alone in autumn woods
six months before that April
morning. Rabid boy, weapon-
heavy craven shit, rightly
despise your weakness, and,
despising, end it. Cock your
beloved gun, cock and lift it.

ANNIVERSARY

Though lovers be lost love shall not;
And death shall have no dominion.
—Dylan Thomas

Two things make you tolerable now,
dumb stone I never met, never knew existed,
have hated now for one full year. The ignominy,

first, of whatever obscure hole gnaws you,
grave without a marker, marker without
a name, cardboard box of cremains

in the back of the closet, not to be
spoken of. Second, the spring of 2008.
Look around, what twisted wraith

there is left of you—mist scuttling
among the scythed necks of corn,
writhing off the New River's wintergreen

willow-shrouded pools, or leaves
dervishing in Drill Field wind,
a rant and a snarl self-banished

from any hope of human hearing—

M

look at them, how the blossoms
survive you. All over campus,

youth unpeels, blithe and forgetful.
By Burruss, daffodils are singing their Star-
of-David suns. By Shultz, the serviceberry

shakes out its fragile snow-flurries.
The fragrant constellations of star magnolia
seethe white-hot by McBryde.

By Norris Hall, towering above your end,
the tulip trees' buds pop like chartreuse
champagne, the sheen of new leaves

curls from dead-gray finger-bone twig tips.
You who were silenced, who did your worst
to silence what suns gunmetal could,

what dominion has your trigger-finger
now, what force your greedy nothingness?
They are not lost, these lovers.

April's joy glitters new grass like sweaty gold.
Below, in earth's grieving black, rich nets of roots
spread and strengthen, in utter silence interlock.

STAR MAGNOLIA, A CELTIC TATTOO

(for Katie Fallon)

Next week, invasion of the media, campus commemorations
on the anniversary of the massacre. Today,

this young man sitting on a bench by McBryde,
smoking a cigarette, waiting for the bus. I study him silently

as I would a sonnet or a landscape, though perhaps with more
focused fervor. Thick black hair and black goatee, beefy build,

just my type, he's smouldering in shorts and muscle shirt,
Celtic tattoo a complex knot along his thick left biceps.

Killing is far from him, EMT boots sole-soaked in blood,
cell phones buzzing inside body bags. The classrooms

where so many were slaughtered are half a block, near a year
distant. For half a minute I stand in his warm breeze, own him,

bind him, while star magnolias scatter the sidewalk
  with sunbursts,
April's white. I rub my silvery chin, wonder how his
  armpits smell,

how his fur-framed mouth tastes, how thick and dark
  his belly hair
might be. Here's surrogacy, the perfumed slow
  collapse of magnolia

blossoms pressed against my face as I turn away from
  him.
Here's spring—here, not there; now, not then—
  handsome,

ignorant, every sweetness sheer luck has spared from
  sacrifice.

Four

ACHILLES AND PATROCLUS

Tomorrow.
Tomorrow, Patroclus.
It is fine armor, and you shall wear it.

Now, though,
do as you have always done.
Roast me the meat of the ox,

warm the rough bread,
dapple it with wild honey. Pour
into goblets, gifts of my father,

the piney wine you brought
from home. Bathe later,
I will bathe you. But now I love

the musk of courage,
the weary scent of you,
black hair like waves as yet unbroken

about your face, across
your breast. How many years
have feasts meant only you and I?

Our couch in firelight,

M

limbs intertwined, drowsy
weight of you, beard brushing my back.

There is blood
on your brow. Kisses
of my mouth will cleanse you.

No, no more
weapons today. I promise
tomorrow. Must the son of a sea goddess

say *Please*?
Strength loves strength.
Who can stand against our arms?

After meat
and wine, close the tent flap.
What is sweetest is your sweat,

fur-salt I lap,
dark sea-way that leads
a warrior home. Such thick arms,

such small wrists.
Inside you I feel blood-
honey, blossom, stone. One day

these partings will depart.
Someone will chant our names,
remember our oath to lie in earth together—

leg bones, ribs
and skulls, these fingers
clasping your still-warm wrist.

Our wedding waits in the dark,

stained with fire, stained with wine.
Bone-urn befitting heroes, forever's graven gold.

ℳ
MUMMY CASE—
FITZWILLIAM
MUSEUM,
CAMBRIDGE

(for Jeremy Maule)

Containing a young man,

Ptolemaic Era, his portrait
painted in an oval on

the wood directly above the dark
where his long-shriveled, sunken face

now rests. The sad wide eyes
of the painting meet mine—sapphire

amidst the curly aureole of black hair,
above full lips and inky beard.

Asp? Dagger? Swamp fever?
His back—the smooth brown

sheen of the Nile his nakedness
swam upon, in desert dusk

as Sirius rose. His sweat—the scent
of cumin and of myrrh. The fur

upon his breast—an ebony
moss, the black between the stars,

within which fortunate lovers
buried their faces, lost themselves

in his life's few years.

GLOUCESTER CATHEDRAL

(for Jeremy Maule)

No one wanted the body.
Deposed, imprisoned, raped
with a hot poker in Berkeley Castle,

screams scalding the surrounding town
like boiling oil. A sodomite's death.
From church to church the corpse was carted,

as if infectious, was bluntly refused, till
one brave bishop opened the doors
of Gloucester Cathedral. Some pilgrim

has been here before me. On a narrow ledge
before Edward's effigy, a few yellow wildflowers
droop. I light a candle, fill out a prayer

request. *Pray for Edward the Second,
who was born too soon.* Who will stroke
the glistening crown, the curly hair

and beard, who will stroke the brow,
comfort the dead, save them
from their deaths? Above the tomb,

the marble canopy's carved

like codified flame ascending.
In a nearby pew, a young man

and woman sit, threatened by no one,
gazing down the gray nave, their hands
joined in stained-glass sunlight.

CERNUNNOS TATTOO

Walpurgisnacht, and tonight on the Brocken
the folk gather, dancing about the bonfire,
sipping ale and May wine, passing about
pumpernickel and wursts, falling together
into carnal grass.

          In Blacksburg, Virginia, I strip
to the waist, slide into Shaun's chair.
Against my left shoulder he presses
the stencil, and then the needles begin.

          Now I am standing
on that Dorset hillside, in silence admiring
the Giant of Cerne Abbas. I stay on my side
of the protective fence, though what I want
is to lie naked in the grass, upon the Giant's erect
    penis,
gripping my own.

          And here, at Cluny, the altar
they found below Notre Dame. Cut in the stone,
the name CERNUNNOS. No museum guard
is looking, so I touch the god's bearded face, the stag
antlers, the brow, my hand shaking and tingling.

And there,
in the books, photos of the Gundestrup Cauldron,
the Lord of the Animals, cross-legged among
deer, clutching a serpent with ram's horns.

    And now here,
in my shoulder's skin. Shaun dips the bee-buzz
needles into tiny pots of black, outlining
the beard, the cheekbones, the antler-spread,

    and my own beard
thickens, the dark hair feathers and spreads, soft
as new spruce needles, over my chest, my belly, my
    groin.
High wind rushes through the antlers of the oak,
the marriage of May Eve, God's face
etched into my animal flesh,
Cernunnos entering the body of His priest.

HEAVEN'S HEARTH

I was Faust once,
addicted to demons—

their red-ember eyes,
their hairy black blandishments.

Saved, I find myself here,
stroking your seraphic brow,

napping by oak-log fire as sleet taps
its tacks against the windowpanes.

I have had to learn the hard way
how to love

the good, the men
from whose shoulders sprout

not membranous arcs of smoke,
but these rainbow wings

that fold about me as we drowse.
Aging, the woes collect,

those migratory sludge-gray birds

where monarchs used to roost.

Tonight, oh every night,
sad slug-trail headlights.

A funeral slides up the street,
the urns are filling with ash.

Provisional blessings
spare us still—hearthside,

listening to heart's beat, listening
to sleet, curled together

in the brevities
between blaze and freeze.

HONEYS

I don't know what to call it.
Not that insanity I've felt for others—lesser men,
your predecessors—
madness I admittedly miss. I've never learned how
to speak well
and passionately about something other than
rapture and sorrow,
those romantic specialties. Each attachment's
a different chemical
amalgam, a different honey hived in the wax cells
of heart and brain.
One season, clover's predominant; another season,
wildflower, sourwood,
basswood, heather, or the mountain laurel,
    hallucinogenic.
I don't know
how to make art from comfort, how to love
what's kind, accessible,
when there's no point to my fangs,
scars and rage.
We spend the evening cooking for one another,
then settle
onto the couch, listen to music,
sip Sambuca,
while freezing rain coats car hoods, somewhere

M

someone else
curses, catches sleet on his lips, sleeps alone,
yearns.
All night I will dream beside you, boat drifting
on the dark
sea-swell of breath, wake to stroke your honey-
blond goatee
in winter-morning light. For a time, it is my time
to be moderate,
to rejoice in learning something new.

OASIS

There are no poems here,
only coconut fried shrimp
with pineapple dipping sauce,

plumeria fluming
orange and pink,
vivid as flame charring

the fingers of the dead.
On the top deck of the Oasis,
we lie naked all morning

in sun's hibiscus-flare.
Midafternoon, hot tub
bubbles finger our thighs,

rainbows glitter
in our chest hair,
piña colada boys breeze by,

serving weak drinks
we doctor with coconut rum.
Midnight, we kiss beneath

arches of banana leaves

shredded by years of storm,
the warm water steams around us.

Your mouth ranging over me,
I lean back into the light
of waxing moon's

pale grapefruit, tropical stars.
Wind's the only lyric,
rustling dryly in palms.

MALLORY SQUARE

Deathbed of aquamarine, bridal train of bronze—
we come to share the sun's theatric daily demise,

to watch trained cats leap through hoops,
clumsy acrobats chuck about on stilts.

Perfectly still, men painted white
pose as toga-draped statues,

as if that flesh deemed
most beautiful the gods might make

marble. A sunset-crowd of hundreds,
and here we all reach the end

of something: this blue-brine
extremity, this island edge.

Behind mangrove keys, to applause
the sun sinks off the Isle of Bones,

this erstwhile Indian graveyard become
rum-rich Eden. Long and lingering

the horizon billows

with crematory fire.

Where do we go from here?
Back to a yearning for more,

knowing more will not satisfy?
The crowd disperses in twilight

chill, the sea goes gray as ash.
On the dock-edge, you hold

my hand, we name
what constellations we can.

THE SEXIEST MAN IN EUROPE

is sipping beer in Delft's town square.
Two tables over, lovers on vacation,
we study the cathedral's facade, try

to read the menu, try not to stare.
He's in his mid-twenties: close-cropped goatee,
bulging biceps, honey-blond hair.

Against his shirtfront glitters a golden necklace.
When next he strips and slips into a shower,
oh, to be links in that chain that we might touch

that chest. Now we're discussing three-ways
and slipknots, converting guilders' rent into dollars,
till the food arrives and we're filling our mouths

with *poffertjes*, little Dutch pancakes heaped
with cherries, gobs of butter, powdered sugar,
whipped cream. Finally, to our relief, he stands,

flexes inside a skin-tight T-shirt his torso's
theophany, takes one last swig of beer, and leaves.
On the hungry way home, we buy from a street-stand

frites met mayo, we stop at a shop to pick up dinner:

pepper paté, cumin-stippled Gouda, oil-cured olives, marinated artichokes, sun-dried-tomato tapanade.

HOMOMONUMENT, AMSTERDAM

*Commemorates all women and men
ever oppressed and persecuted
because of their homosexuality.*

Pink triangles of granite.
    Three of them, interlocked,
        jutting out into the busy waters

of Keizersgracht. A smooth
    stone shelf we step onto
        gingerly, as if it were an edge

of rosy ice that might break loose
    and floe us off to sea. About our feet,
        white wreaths of lilies, peony-

scatter, wilting commemorations
    like those rose bouquets tenderly
        laid about the statue of Anne Frank

just around the corner. Here, flowers
    share the space with cigarette ends,
        bottle caps, candle butts, the pearly swirls

of wax long cooled. (Semen's

molten moonstone sealing together
        the bellies of lucky lovers, tears freezing

a widower's beard.) In a safety
    born of sheer coincidence, on this pink
        promontory flanked by the canal's

wake and flux, we touch history's
    spilled tallow, calla lily memories
        not our own: the lesbian stoned to death

in the public square, the faggot-
    pyre heaped about the sodomite,
        ashes shoveled from the cooling

furnaces of Buchenwald.
    Those deaths become our whetstone.
        Upon this pink granite prow sword-sharp

and sheer as honed will,
    we sit together, knee to knee,
        in the Dutch sun's imprimatur,

dipping *frites* into mayonnaise,
    feeding each another.
        Perfect photo opportunity for those

in tour boats who float by. They listen to
    the story of the Homomonument, point us out—
        living examples!—aim their cameras, smile.

THE BELLS OF BRUGES

There is no chamber pot to hurl.
Not a lack I would normally feel,

but this sleep-splintering clamor in the street,
this corbie-stepped setting suddenly put me

in mind of it. Such an easily lobbable item,
such a nastily simple way to express displeasure.

The earth is beautiful, its people
unaccommodating. Like Juvenal,

I hurl words instead, or would if
I could bring myself to leave our bed.

We've had a busy tourist-morning—
a climb up the bell tower, a boat tour

along medieval canals. For lunch, crepes
with *advocaat*, then this midafternoon nap.

Which returns me to the chamber pot,
the inconvenient absence of it.

Children are shrieking in the street below

Mour open window, garbage cans ruckus by.

One reason to hate humanity:
the way it mars near-perfect moments.

I am annoyed, half-awake, my snarl
only another marring, but your soft snores

keep course through it all, till a sudden hard rain
empties the street, till there is only

the shush of it, pewter simmering on the sill,
a veil chimes part at intervals.

Only bells and rain now, your breath and mine.
My chin on your clavicle, chest hair

tickling my nose, I watch the pulse beat
metronomic in the curve of your neck.

By my mother's deathbed I watched
the drum skin loosen, the heart unwind.

Today, sweet steadiness of youth,
your nakedness curls against mine,

the bells of your blood do not falter,
joining the distant carillons of Bruges,

opening their silver flowers,
tonguing melodies I cannot name.

ACKNOWLEDGMENTS

Many thanks to the editors of the following journals and anthologies, in which many of these poems first appeared.

Knockout: "Mummy Case—Fitzwilliam Museum, Cambridge," "Gloucester Cathedral," and "4x4"
White Crane: "Achilles and Patroclus" and "Heaven's Hearth"
Appalachian Heritage: "Locrian," " Ionian," "Mixolydian," "Lydian," "Dorian," "Aeolian," "Phrygian," "Single Men," and "Milkweed Pods in November"
The Southern Poetry Anthology, Volume III: Contemporary Appalachia, edited by Jesse Graves, Paul Ruffin, and William Wright: "Locrian"
ABZ: "Sycamore"
Chiron Review: "The Bells of Bruges"
Spoon River Poetry Review: "The Men of Taco Bell" and "Grendel"
Bayou: "Sugar Maples in October"
Crab Orchard Review: "Galatoire's"
West Branch: "Weekend"
The Poet's Domain: "Snow Meal"
WormWood Review: "Erotic Letter" and "Mysteries"
Amethyst: "Getting a Piece"
Kestrel: "Graveyard Maples After Sleet" and "Lunar Eclipse"

His Underwear, edited by Todd Gregory: "Relic"
Best Gay Poetry 2008, edited by Lawrence Schimel: "Relic"
Poetic Voices without Borders, edited by Robert L. Giron: "Oasis"
Poetic Voices without Borders 2, edited by Robert L. Giron: "Honeys"
The Pagan's Muse: Words of Ritual, Invocation, and Inspiration, edited by Jane Raeburn: "Cernunnos Tattoo"
Collective Brightness: LGBTIQ Poets on Faith, Religion and Spirituality, edited by Kevin Simmonds: "Cernunnos Tattoo"
Midnight Mind Number Two, or The Guide to Safe Camping, edited by Brett Van Emst: "Mallory Square"
Key West: A Collection, edited by Brett Van Emst: "Mallory Square"
I Do/I Don't: Queers on Marriage, edited by Greg Wharton and Ian Philips: "Virginia Fantasia"
Echoes from the Heart: An Anthology of Poetry for Peace: "September Morning Fog"
Coal: A Poetry Anthology, edited by Chris Green: "Black Windows" and "Locrian"
Blue Fifth Review: "Greg's Party," "Three Crosses," and "Writers' Tour of Kayford Mountain"
Prairie Schooner: "Sheath"
Willow Springs: "Sunday Morning Biscuits"
Anthology of Appalachian Writers: "Feasting in the Aftermath"
Arts and Letters: "Star Magnolias, a Celtic Tattoo"
The Lambda Literary Review: "The Sexiest Man in Europe"
Chelsea Station: "Homomonument, Amsterdam" and "Alan Turing Memorial— Manchester"

JEFF MANN grew up in Covington, Virginia, and Hinton, West Virginia, receiving degrees in English and forestry from West Virginia University. His poetry, fiction, and essays have appeared in many publications, including *Arts and Letters, Prairie Schooner, Shenandoah, Willow Springs, The Gay and Lesbian Review Worldwide, Crab Orchard Review,* and *Appalachian Heritage.* He has published three award-winning poetry chapbooks, *Bliss, Mountain Fireflies,* and *Flint Shards from Sussex*; three full-length books of poetry, *Bones Washed with Wine, On the Tongue,* and *Ash: Poems from Norse Mythology*; two collections of personal essays, *Edge: Travels of an Appalachian Leather Bear* and *Binding the God: Ursine Essays from the Mountain South*; two novellas, *Devoured,* included in *Masters of Midnight: Erotic Tales of the Vampire,* and *Camp Allegheny,* included in *History's Passion: Stories of Sex Before Stonewall*; two novels, *Fog: A Novel of Desire and Reprisal,* which won the Pauline Réage Novel Award, and *Purgatory: A Novel of the Civil War,* which won a Rainbow Award; a book of poetry and memoir, *Loving Mountains, Loving Men*; and two volumes of short fiction, *Desire and Devour: Stories of Blood and Sweat* and *A History of Barbed Wire,* which won a Lambda Literary Award. He teaches creative writing at Virginia Tech in Blacksburg, Virginia.

CPSIA information can be obtained at www.ICGtesting.com
Printed in the USA
BVOW082346040413

317355BV00002B/2/P